THE WAY OF THE SPIRIT

Bible Reading Course Workbook

Part 3

HEIRS OF THE PROPHETS

John McKay

Kingdom Faith

Published in Great Britain by
Kingdom Faith Trust, Horsham, West Sussex

Copyright © 1990 John McKay

All rights reserved. No part of this publication may be reproduced, stored in a retrieval system, or transmitted, in any form or by any means, electronic, mechanical, photocopying, recording or otherwise, without the permission in writing, of Kingdom Faith Trust.

Scripture in all four parts of
The Way of the Spirit taken from the
HOLY BIBLE, NEW INTERNATIONAL VERSION.
Copyright © 1973, 1978, 1984 by
International Bible Society. Used by
permission of Hodder and Stoughton Limited.

ISBN: 1-900409-05-4

Typeset in Times Roman by Kingdom Faith Trust.

The Way of the Spirit Bible Reading Course is administered through Kingdom Faith Trust, Registered Charity No. 278746.

To order further copies of this workbook, or the textbook and tapes that go with it, or for any information about *The Way of the Spirit*, or details of other literature, or any matters related to it, contact:

The Way of the Spirit, Roffey Place, Old Crawley Road,
Faygate, Horsham, West Sussex RH12 4RU.
Tel: 01293 851543. Fax: 01293 854610. E-mail: info@thewayofthespirit.com
Web Site: http://www.thewayofthespirit.com

THE WAY OF THE SPIRIT

A Bible Reading Course

Part 3

HEIRS OF THE PROPHETS

Welcome to The Way of the Spirit Bible Reading Course.

The pages you are holding outline a six-month course of Bible study based on a textbook, *The Way of the Spirit, A Bible Reading Guide and Commentary, Vol. 3: Heirs of the Prophets*, distributed through Kingdom Faith.

This is actually Part Three of a fuller course made up of four parts altogether, but while it links naturally with the other parts, it is not written simply as a follow-on or introduction to any of them. Each part is a self-contained unit.

Although you may use this outline prayerfully on its own, it is designed primarily as a weekly workbook to accompany the reading guide, supported by a set of six teaching tapes each containing four 20 minute talks relating to the week's readings.

Used together the textbook, tapes and workbook make an integrated study programme for a one-term course at Kingdom Faith Bible College, where students use this workbook to direct their daily study and the textbook for background information, while the tapes contain their lectures in condensed form.

Aim of the Course

The aim is quite simply to help you better understand the way of God's Spirit in the Scriptures. The sort of questions we shall concentrate on are:

- What God has been doing down the full sweep of history, so that we can align ourselves with his plans and purposes.
- What God has done in the lives of individuals down the centuries, so that we can appreciate what he can do in us.
- What God has offered to do for us, so that we can learn to have fuller faith in his promises.
- What he has asked us to do for him, so that we can learn better what it is to obey him.
- What God has done in Jesus, and what the significance of that is for us.

My prayer is that through your reading and praying you will enter yourself into the fullness of life that men of Bible-times experienced and that God still offers us today.

The Content and Theme of the Course

Our aim is to cover the history and teaching of the prophets from the time of Samuel on, tracing the part they played in Israel's revivals, studying their warnings of judgment, examining their vision of the future, and seeing how their hope and experience came alive again in Christ's ministry and in the life of the early Church.

The books of the Bible you will be studying are therefore mainly the historical and prophetic ones, plus selected passages from Acts and Paul's letters:

    OT: 1 Samuel – 2 Kings, Isaiah – Malachi.
    NT: Luke, Acts, Corinthians, Revelation.

The great themes you will find yourself most frequently discussing are prophecy and revival, judgment and repentance, vision and hope, the work of the Spirit, Jesus as Prophet and the Church as charismatic.

Plan of Study

The study-plan corresponds exactly with the arrangement of the textbook:

1. An opening survey of the Bible's story up to the time of Samuel as background to the story of the prophets (Genesis – Judges; week 1).
2. The early prophets from Samuel to Elisha and their work for revival (1 Samuel – 2 Kings; weeks 2–3).
3. The 8th c. prophets, the Assyrians and the fall of Samaria (Amos, Hosea, Micah, Isaiah; weeks 4–8).
4. The 7th–6th c. prophets and Jerusalem's fall to the Babylonians (Jeremiah, Zephaniah, Nahum, Obadiah, Habakkuk, Ezekiel; weeks 9–15).
5. The visions of the restoration prophets (Isaiah 40–66, Haggai, Zechariah, Joel, Malachi; weeks 16–18).
6. The rebirth of prophecy in Jesus' ministry and the growth of prophetic/charismatic Christianity (Luke, Acts, Paul; weeks 19–21).
7. The final prophetic vision of the future (Revelation; weeks 22–23).

What you will get out of this course

You should certainly end up with a better understanding of your Bible and of God's working by the Spirit in you, which is, of course, the primary aim of the course.

It is possible to take this course with assistance by correspondence and receive a certificate of completion, but Paul reminds us in 2 Cor. 3.3 that the gospel of our Lord Jesus Christ is not about writing with ink on paper, but about writing that the Spirit does on our hearts. If you are prepared to let him do such writing on your heart as you study your Bible you will receive a better certificate than any man can give you.

May the good Lord bless you richly as you study his Word.

John McKay

For further information please write to:

The Way of the Spirit, Roffey Place, Old Crawley Road,
Faygate, Horsham, West Sussex RH12 4RU.
Tel: 01293 851543. Fax: 01293 854610. E-mail: info@thewayofthespirit.com

Or visit our web site at **http://www.thewayofthespirit.com**

METHODS OF STUDY

There are several different ways in which you can follow this course:

1. Using only this workbook and your Bible.
2. Using only this workbook, the textbook and your Bible.
3. Using workbook, textbook, tapes and Bible.
4. Using workbook, textbook, tapes and Bible, with extra help by correspondence.
5. Using workbook, textbook, tapes and Bible, studying along with others in a group.

Whichever method you adopt, there are certain principles you should keep in mind in order to get full benefit from the course:

1. You will need to commit yourself to a programme of regular daily prayer, Bible reading and course study.
2. As you read your Bible, keep your mind open to hear what the Holy Spirit has to tell you. Allow him to speak to you personally through its pages about your own beliefs, attitudes and life-style.
3. Watch carefully for what God does and says, and for how the men of Old and New Testament times respond to him, because that is what the way of the Spirit is all about.
4. And don't forget to keep asking yourself what lessons you should be learning from their experience, so that you can apply them to your own life as a Christian, to help you grow into maturity of faith.

Using the workbook

An introductory paragraph stands at the head of each week's readings telling you about the main themes of the week's study and giving some general advice on how to approach it.

The passages for daily study usually have two questions attached to each of them, the first of which tends to be (though not always) more factual and the second more personal.

The small space left between these questions is there to give you a rough indication of the length your answers should be and to impress on you that in answering them you should watch for the main point in what you are reading and express yourself pointedly in a few words or phrases without rambling on wastefully.

At the end of each week's readings there are some review questions. They are partly for revision purposes, but also to determine what you have learned from your reading and to encourage you to consider how to apply that to your life as a Christian.

Using the textbook

If you are using this workbook along with the textbook, you will find answers to some of the questions in it, but not to all of them. The primary purpose of the textbook is to provide background information and to point out the main drift of the way of the Spirit so that you can read the Bible meaningfully for yourself. *It is not in any way a substitute for reading the Bible and listening to the Spirit,* but only something to help you to do that more meaningfully for yourself.

At the start of each week read the relevant pages in the textbook (see top right of each weekly section in this workbook), so that you get an outline of the story and its background before you begin your week's study, and then glance through the same pages again at the end of the week.

You will also find it helpful to use in conjunction with your daily readings, and you should certainly keep referring to its maps and charts to see how everything fits together.

Using the tapes

If you are using the tapes, listen to the introductory talk before you start your first week's study. That explains further what the course is about and how to use it. Then do your week's reading, then listen to the next talk, and so on.

You may find it helpful to listen to each tape before you start your week's reading, but if you do so you should also listen to it again at the end of the week, because the commentary on the tapes often assumes that you have already read the relevant passages.

Assistance by correspondence

Some people find it difficult to sustain study on their own without help and encouragement. You could get that by doing the course along with a friend or in a group, or alternatively we can arrange for you to be linked with someone with whom you can correspond. His or her job will not be to teach (the teaching is done by the published materials), but to encourage, direct and advise, to -

  (a) monitor your progress by reading your worksheets,
  (b) give you some direction and encouragement in your studies,
  (c) be your personal link to help you grow in the Spirit.

If you would like to be put in contact with such a person, or would simply like more information about how the system works, please write to us. Whoever you are linked with will then make arrangements privately for corresponding with you.

Study in a group

This is by far the most satisfactory way of doing the course. Discussion and mutual support do much to sustain enthusiasm and provide additional enlightenment.

Group meetings will vary according to their members' needs, but should include time for prayer and fellowship, as well as for hearing the taped talk about the week's study, discussing answers to the questions, sharing insights and encouraging one another to grow in the Lord.

The duration of the course

As it is set out, the course should take just under six months to complete. You may, however, prefer to work more slowly and spread each weekly reading over a fortnight, or perhaps, if you can cope with the pace, to do two weeks work in one each time, as the students at Roffey do. You must work out the programme that suits you best, whether you have assistance by correspondence or not.

There is a reason for the weekly division as it stands: to encourage you to treat this as a *reading* course, rather than a detailed, analytical study. Tackle your daily readings in something like the way you might read a novel, to get the flow and feel of the story.

You will probably need to lay aside about 30 mins. every day, so that you can pray, read, think and answer the questions. Try this method, or something like it:

- Pray for about five minutes.
- Look at the questions in this workbook.
- Read your set portion of Scripture.
- Think about what you have read.
- Ask the Lord to make it living for you.
- Answer the questions.

Remember that you will require more time, possibly an extra half-hour, on the first or last day of the week, so that you can look at the textbook and listen to the tape.

The time is, of course, less important than that you enjoy the course and learn to listen to God's Word and his Spirit speaking to you through what you read. It is a good idea to look for some key sentence daily, write it down, and commit it to memory. Let God's word become part of you, whether that takes you three months, six months or a year. But be careful not to become sloppy in your approach. Do try to exercise some discipline and become regular in your study. You will find yourself richly rewarded.

Week 1   Heirs of the Prophets, Pages 17–32

THE BIRTH OF PROPHECY IN ISRAEL

This first week's readings are simply to set the background. The first four provide a summary of God's plan, promises and requirements for the life of his people to which the prophets constantly appeal. The next two outline the conditions of decadence that preceded the birth of prophecy. The last two introduce us to the nature of prophecy.

....

Gen. 12: God's word of promise revealed to Abraham.
   What did God say he would do through Abraham and his descendants?

   How did Abraham respond to God's plan and how should I be responding to it now?

Exod. 20: God's word of command revealed to Moses.
   What kind of life-style does God require for his people?

   How far do I live up to it?

Deut. 30: Disobedience and the possibility of repentance.
   What are the consequences of obedience, disobedience and repentance?

   What lessons have you learned through your own acts of obedience, disobedience and repentance?

Josh. 24: Faith in God's word is vindicated.
   What are the terms of God's covenant with his people outlined by Joshua?

   Can you today renew your own covenant with God on the basis of these terms?

Judg. 2.1 – 3.6: Spiral of decline and deliverance.
Israel's sin was identifying with the ways of the pagans around them. With what consequences? (See 2.20 – 3.4)

How far are you turning away from God's ways and identifying with the ways of the world? The consequences are likely to be the same.

Judg. 19–21: Plunge into anarchy.
How would you describe the state of the nation at the end of the period of the judges?

Do you see any similarities between the problems of society then and today? What do you think the Lord's solution to them might be?

Deut. 18.14-22: The prophets' vocation.
What do these verses tell you about the function of prophecy?

How do today's prophets measure up in the light of this passage?

Num. 22–24: A prophet of the nations.
How did God make the pagan Balaam one who would speak his words?

What does 24.1-4 tell you about the work of the Spirit in prophetic revelation?

....

REVIEW

God calls us to faith in his promises about his purpose for our world (Gen. 12), to obedience to his commands that will make us the kind of people we need to be for fulfilling his purpose (Exod. 20), and to repentance when we fail (Deut. 30). Have you responded to his call and renewed your covenant with him this week (Josh. 24)?

Turning away from God can have disastrous consequences (Judges), but God always provides someone who will speak for him as Moses did, to lead us back to God (Deut. 18). Whose voice do you heed?

Week 2 *Heirs of the Prophets, Pages 34–46*

ISRAEL'S FIRST PROPHETIC MOVEMENT AND REVIVAL (1 Samuel)

Israel's first prophetic movement was born out of need for revival. It summoned the Lord's people to return to him in repentance, which led to an upsurge of religious enthusiasm, but also resulted in some very radical social and political changes. As you read its story, see if you can find any parallels with our present-day charismatic movements that have brought a resurgence of faith to many of our churches.

....

Chs. 1–2: Samuel's infancy and youth.
What are the evidences of decadence in the Israel of Samuel's childhood?

What was God's attitude to this decadence and what was he doing about it?

Chs. 3–4: His call to be a prophet and the fall of Shiloh.
What connection do you see between the visit of the man of God in ch. 2 and Samuel's call?

Samuel was raised up for revival, but God did not grant it immediately. He allowed the judgment of ch. 4 first. Why?

Chs. 7–8: Revival breaks out.
Samuel's revival needed a life-time of continuous hard work. Do we too easily expect instant miracles today?

Was it God's will that Samuel's leadership should be replaced by Saul's? Should revivalists have to hand over to a kingdom-builder?

Chs. 9–10: Israel is given a prophet-king.
Why should Saul have had to receive the Spirit and become a prophet/charismatic before he could take over from Samuel?

What similarities do you see between the activities of Samuel's prophets in ch. 10 and the practices of today's charismatics?

Chs. 11–12: Saul's coronation and first faith challenge.
In ch. 11 the Spirit gave Saul the courage to act. Have you ever had a similar experience?

What does Samuel's sermon in ch. 12 tell you about the function of prophecy? What relevance does that have for you today?

Chs. 15–16; 19.18-24: Samuel, Saul, David, the prophets and the Spirit.
If Samuel was so angry at Saul's rebellion and arrogance, why did he mourn for him (15.35)?

What similarities do you see between the activities of Samuel's prophets in ch. 19 and the practices of today's charismatics?

2 Sam. 7 & 11–12: God's promise to David and his rebuke.
Summarise God's promise to David.

What lessons do you draw from David's reaction to the prophetic word in ch. 12?

....

REVIEW

What have you learned this week about revival? About:

– How to get it.

– The role of prophetic men in it.

– Its purpose.

– Its impact.

– What spoils it.

– The place of today's prophetic/charismatic movements in it.

ELIJAH, ELISHA AND THE SONS OF THE PROPHETS
(1 Kings 17 – 2 Kings 13)

The readings are quite long this week. Though shorter than you would tackle if reading a novel, you may find it easier to spread them over two weeks. Take yourself in imagination into the stories. See yourself standing alongside Elijah and Elisha. Feel the atmosphere as if you were there with them. And look out for traces of things familiar today. Prophets then were not entirely different from prophets in our time.

....

1 Kings 11.26-40; 12.21-24; 13.1-10; 14.1-18; 16.1-7: Elijah's forerunners in the tenth century.
These prophets all spoke with kings. How would you say they differ from political agitators?

None of them led a national revival. How then do they differ from revivalist prophets, like Samuel?

1 Kings 17–19: Elijah and the start of a second wave of revival.
What attitudes to God and the people did Elijah have that enabled him to trigger off revival? What attitudes hampered him, if any?

How much of yourself do you see in Elijah's reactions to God's word and other people's? What does your answer suggest you need to do?

1 Kings 20–21; 2 Kings 1: The prophetic voice increases and grows in confidence.
What is the evidence that Elijah's ministry was making a continuing impact?

What would you say was Elijah's main strength of personality? Could it also be part of yours?

2 Kings 2–5: Elisha and the 'Sons of the Prophets'.
What picture do you get of life among the prophets?

Can you think of any New Testament or present-day parallels to some of the stories in these chapters?

2 Kings 6–8: Elisha's charismatic ministry continues.

What signs are there here of growing openness to the voice of the prophets at court?

Note the prophets' total involvement in politics and war as well as in homely affairs. How should charismatics approach the full range of society's problems today?

2 Kings 9–10; 13.10-21: The overthrow of Baalism and the end of Elisha's ministry.

Why should people have had such low opinions of the Lord's prophets (9.12) when they actually had a powerful impact for good?

Elisha's ministry secured the continuity of revival, but at the cost of much bloodshed. Do you think that it had to be so?

1 Kings 13 & 22: The problem of true and false prophecy.

How did the man of God from Judah allow himself to be deceived?

What do you learn from these examples about testing prophetic words that are given to you?

....

REVIEW

How would you sum up Elijah's impact on his times?

How would you sum up Elisha's impact on his times?

Prophecy in today's church is very different from the prophecy of these men who lived in times of war and palace intrigue and who themselves made and unmade kings. And yet our prophets/charismatics are still God's shock-troops for revival and do have many traits in common with them.

What would you say are the main similarities between the prophets of Elijah's day and ours?

What would you say are the main differences?

Week 4   *Heirs of the Prophets, Pages 60–69*

WARNINGS OF APPROACHING JUDGMENT (Amos and Hosea)

You will not find many stories in the writings of the prophets, but rather messages and visions they received from God. That sometimes makes reading more difficult. It may be best to look over the relevant pages in your Reading Guide first,to get an overview of the book you are about to study. It will also help if your reading focuses on finding answers to the questions below. You will actually find that the central message in each book is quite simple and straightforward.

....

Amos 1–2: Judgment on the nations and on Israel.
How would you describe the 'sins' of the nations?

How would you describe the 'sins' of Judah and Israel? Were they any worse than the sins of the nations?

Amos 3–5: Look at your record and repent!
What was the nature of God's judgment to be?

How could it be averted?

Amos 6–8: The relentlessness of coming judgment.
What is the main thing Amos says God wants from his people?

What do you learn from ch. 7 about a prophet's vocation?

Amos 9: The judgment and beyond.
The further we read in Amos, the more absolute God's judgment seems to become. What hope does he say there will be and for whom?

Does restoration and blessing always have to be preceded by judgment on sin? Is there no other way?

Hos. 1–3: Hosea's prophetic marriage.
What was the main lesson God taught Hosea through his marriage?

What did he learn about Israel's hope for the future?

Hos. 4: The main reasons for God's disgust.
How were Israel's leaders to blame for the rot in society?

What lessons do you draw for Christian ministry today?

Hos. 5–7: An extended plea for repentance.
What good did God want for his people?

Why could he not give it?

....

REVIEW

Amos preached God's desire for social justice, Hosea God's mixed anger and compassion. Both were addressing basically the same society at roughly the same time. Whose preaching would you feel better suited to today's social conditions? Why?

They also had strong things to say about the religion of their day (e.g. Amos 5.21-4; Hos. 4.4-19). How much of that remains relevant in our churches today?

Many people think prophets preach only judgment, all doom and gloom. What else did you find these two preaching?

What have you learned about the cost of being a prophet this week? Do Spirit-filled Christians still face the same cost in our own time?

GOD'S ANGER AND HIS COMPASSION (Hosea and Micah)

The basic message of all prophecy is 'Repent or face the consequence', but each prophet expresses that differently. Hosea spoke about wrong heart attitudes, Micah about wrong theological presuppositions, that is as well as many other sins. Both agreed God's desire is to show mercy, though not at the expense of justice. He cannot allow sin to multiply unchecked, and without repentance or a change of heart, he must judge. Watch for the different ways they express this message.

....

Hos. 8–10: The consequences Israel can expect as the result of her sin.
What were the evidences that Israel's protestations of acknowledging God were sham?

How would you apply 10.12 to your own personal situation today?

Hos. 11: A Father's love for his son.
Summarise the story of Israel's relationship with God, past and future, as outlined in this chapter.

What does this chapter tell you about the Father-heart of God?

Hos. 12–14: A final plea for repentance.
What would you say was the root cause of Israel's sin?

What does ch. 14 tell you about the nature and power of repentance?

Mic. 1: God's judgment on Samaria and Jerusalem.
Note the scene has changed. Amos and Hosea prophesied in the North, Micah in Jerusalem. What difference does that make for his message?

What is the judgment Micah foresees?

Mic. 2–3: Greedy leaders and false prophets.

What is the sin of Jerusalem's leaders? Where is it still a problem today?

What is the sin of Jerusalem's prophets? Where is that still a problem?

Mic. 4–5: 'Now' and 'in the last days'.

How will God use the Assyrians and Babylonians in bringing judgment?

What is God's ultimate purpose for Zion/Jerusalem?

Mic. 6–7 God's compassion and Israel's ingratitude.

How would you summarise the message of ch. 6?

What does ch. 7 tell us about God's heart towards his people?

....

REVIEW

Both Hosea and Micah reveal to us the heart of God full of love and compassion towards his people, though equally full of anger against injustice and corruption. Which passages in both books best summed that up for you?

Which passages best summed up what our attitude to him should be?

What was there in Hosea's message that you felt should still be heard in our churches today?

And what in Micah's?

What was the remnant and why should there be one (Mic. 2.12; 5.7f; 7.18)?

What does Mic. 2–3 teach you about testing true and false prophecy?

Week 6   *Heirs of the Prophets, Pages 79–90*

THE CHALLENGE OF HOLINESS AND FAITH (Isaiah 1–12)

No prophet taught faith as Isaiah did; there is much we can learn from him. God gave him such an overwhelming revelation of his holiness that he knew it was never right to fear or trust anyone save God alone. But he was no abstract philosopher. Faith had to work in the hard realities of life, and in the crises of war. To get the full flavour of his teaching you will need to know something of the historical context. Your Reading Guide will help you with that.

Chs. 1–2: Seek justice.
List some of the echoes of Amos', Hosea's or Micah's teaching you see here.

What is Isaiah saying that God asks of us?

3.1 – 4.1 & ch. 5: God's verdict on Jerusalem.
What does the song of the vineyard in 5.1-7 tell you about how God relates to his own people (today, the Church)?

The sins in chs. 3 & 5 still stir God's anger. What then can we learn from Isaiah and so escape judgment in our own time?

Ch. 6: The Holy One of Israel and the Holy Remnant.
You will never have the same particular experience, but you can have the same essential experience of God as in vv. 1-8. Read these verses through several times. Imagine yourself there with Isaiah in the temple, and pray that God will reveal his glory to you too.

Have you ever felt that your witnessing has the same effect as Isaiah was told his would have in vv. 9-13? If so, why? (Cp. Mark 4.11f.)

Chs. 7–8: Faith in a crisis.
You will only grasp the full impact of the message here if you lay hold of the basic historical setting. What particular promise of God should Ahaz have been trusting?

What encouragement for faith in your own life do you draw from these chapters? What promise of God should you be trusting today?

Chs. 9.8 – 10.34: Assyria and Jerusalem.
Why was God's anger not turned away in 9.8 – 10.4?

How did he execute his anger through Assyria in 10.5-34?

4.2-6; 9.1-7; 11.1-9: The Age of Messiah (cp. 32.1-8).
What did Isaiah say Messiah would be like?

What did he say he would do when he comes?

Ch. 12: In that day you will praise the Lord.
In what day? And for what?

How far has the experience for which the Israelites were to give thanks now become yours in Christ?

....

REVIEW

In these chapters Isaiah has spoken several times about 'a remnant' left after judgment to become the nucleus of God's people for the future. Look over these passages again (4.2-6; 7.3; 10.20-23; 11.10-16; cp. 1.24-26; 6.13). See what kind of community the remnant is to be and ask yourself whether your church today is anything like it, whether it should be and how it can become so.

What have you learned about faith this week?

What have you learned about holiness?

What have you learned about God's will for your own life as a Christian?

Week 7   *Heirs of the Prophets, Pages 90–3*

THE WHOLE WORLD AS GOD'S KINGDOM (Isaiah 13–27)

You will find this week's readings quite straight forward if you read their message as addressed to the Lord's people (not the nations), to encourage them to have faith in him rather than run for help to people whose days are numbered anyway. Chs. 13–23 show God in control of both Israel's history and that of all nations. Chs. 24–27 take us into his wider purposes for the more distant future of his own people and all mankind. See what encouragement you derive from these chapters.

....

13.1 – 14.23: Against Babylon.
What encouragement for the Lord's people is there in these chapters?

In 14.12-15 the king of Babylon is compared with the morning star (Latin: Lucifer) which may symbolise Satan. What does his sin and fall have in common with that of the Babylonian king?

14.24 – 16.13: Against Assyria, Philistia and Moab.
What do the two little prophecies about Assyria and Philistia in ch. 14 tell you about God's control over history?

What is God's attitude to Moab reflected in these chapters (see especially 16.1-4)?

Chs. 17–18: Against Damascus and Cush.
What is the faith message in ch. 17? (Compare vv. 10-14 with Ps. 2.)

Why will the people of Cush bring gifts to Zion (18.7, cp. 2.1-5)?

Chs. 19–21: Against Egypt, Cush, Babylon, Edom and Arabia.
What does ch. 19 tell you about God's ultimate purpose for the nations?

Why is Isaiah so opposed to foreign alliances? Do you think he is unrealistic?

Chs. 22–23: Concerning Jerusalem and Tyre.
What was wrong with the people's reaction to the relief of Jerusalem (22.1-16)?

What does the fall of Tyre tell us about our source of security?

Chs. 24–25: On the day of God's end-time visitation.
Why do you think God should plan such devastation for the earth as described in ch. 24?

What does ch. 25 tell us about the blessings the Lord's people can look forward to in the end?

Chs. 26–27: The final gathering of God's people.
How would you summarise the theme of the song in ch. 26?

What does ch. 27 tell us about God's purpose in judging his own people?

....

REVIEW

Some of the disasters to befall the nations seem very harsh, but they certainly accord with historical reality and do accurately reflect man's inhumanity to man. But Isaiah goes one step further and says they are decreed by God for judgment. How would you explain God's justice in executing them?

Does his justice operate in a different way towards his own people? (Cp. ch. 22)

How does God's compassion operate in relation to the nations? (See chs. 15–16, 19, 21.)

What have you learned here about trusting God rather than men?

What personal hope did you derive from Isaiah's portrait of the end-time future of the world?

Week 8   *Heirs of the Prophets, Pages 93–7*

THE TESTING OF FAITH IN A CRISIS (Isaiah 28–39)

The prophecies in the first chapters here relate mainly to the history told in the last four. In them we see prophetic faith put to the test in a very extreme crisis and vindicated. Isaiah's teaching was far from mere idealism; it actually worked. But then it was founded on God's promise, not just on imagination. As you read, keep asking how the principles he outlines might apply in your own situation in life. And watch in particular for the verses that encourage faith: Mark them and learn them.

....

Chs. 28–29: Woe to the city of David.
Faith will never work without repentance and holiness of life. It does not just look at promises without any care for what is wrong. List some of the things Isaiah says need repentance.

Now see whether any of them apply in your life.

What verses in these chapters encourage faith?

Chs. 30–31: Trust in the Lord alone.
What does Isaiah teach here about trusting men?

What does he teach about trusting God?

Chs. 32–33: The coming of God's new kingdom.
What, according to ch. 32, are the two main things that usher in God's blessing?

What kind of people does Isaiah say in ch. 33 will enjoy the blessings of Zion's new age?

Chs. 34–35: Judgment and redemption.
Why do you think the Lord is angry with the nations (ch. 34)?

List some of the blessings the redeemed of the Lord can look forward to.

Chs. 36–37: The deliverance of Jerusalem.
Describe the challenge confronting Hezekiah in ch. 36.

Outline the part faith played in the deliverance of Jerusalem in ch. 37.

Chs. 38–39: And the Davidic King—did he learn faith?
What lessons for faith should Hezekiah have learned through his healing (ch. 38)?

Why was Isaiah so upset in ch. 39?

....

REVIEW

Write out in full some of the verses that struck you as being particularly encouraging for faith.

What will you do when your time of crisis comes—look to men for help, or to God? Whom do you trust most?

Week 9   *Heirs of the Prophets, Pages 99–108*

A CALL FOR REPENTANCE AND A CHANGE OF HEART (Jeremiah 1–13)

We learn Jeremiah's message as much through his personal experiences as through his words. The stories about him are not told just to fill you in on the background of his life, but to teach you God's ways. Watch for the message in them as well as in the prophecies. And watch for the expressions of his own feelings in his prophecies. You will discover a man with emotions and reactions very like your own.

....

Ch. 1: Jeremiah is called to be a prophet.
   How did God encourage the unwilling Jeremiah to take up his ministry?

   What is the gist of the message God gave him to proclaim?

Chs. 2–4: Return to the Lord.
   What is the root cause of Israel's sin as outlined in 2.1 – 3.5?

   If Israel does 'return', what will happen, according to 3.6 – 4.31?

Chs. 5–6: Take heed before it is too late.
   What evidence is there in ch. 5 that the rot has set in deep?

   Ch. 6 warns about invasion, but does it offer any hope?

Chs. 7 & 26: Jeremiah's 'Temple Sermon': Your religion is corrupt and will not save you.
   What was wrong with the people's attitude to the temple?

   Why did the authorities react so strongly to Jeremiah's preaching? Can you think of any biblical or modern parallel's to the story in ch. 26?

Chs. 8–10: No-one repents of his wickedness.
How were the religious authorities of Jeremiah's day tackling national corruption?

How does Jeremiah feel in his own heart about the lack of repentance?

11.1 – 12.4: Jeremiah begins to learn the cost of prophetic ministry.
What kind of response is Jeremiah getting to his ministry?

What is Jeremiah's reaction to that response?

12.5 – 13.27: The Lord sends him back to prophesying.
How would you summarise God's answer to Jeremiah's complaint (12.5-13)?

How would you summarise Jeremiah's prophetic word in ch. 13?

....

REVIEW

Jeremiah frequently sounds desperate about the hardness of men's heart and about their unwillingness to repent (cp. 5.23; 6.10; 8.6,21f). So stubborn is man that he even says it is as impossible for him to change as it is for an Ethiopian to change his skin or a leopard his spots (13.23). From your experience of speaking to people about Christ, have you ever found it to be the same?

Why then did Jeremiah bother to continue prophesying? Why do you think it worth continuing to tell the gospel?

What is God's answer to man's hardness and unrepentance?

How did God encourage Jeremiah in what he found depressing work? How does he encourage you?

What encouragement have you received from Jeremiah's story so far?

Week 10   Heirs of the Prophets, Pages 108–13

CONFRONTATIONS (Jeremiah 14–29)

Jeremiah's ministry, like so many powerful prophetic and preaching ministries of the past and today, angers the religious authorities. Later he suffers at the hands of the political powers as well, but at first it is they who defend him. The churchmen are his main persecutors. The pattern is the same as Jesus and Paul experienced. Look out for the parallels and see if they still apply today.

....

Chs. 14–15: Jeremiah's second experience of persecution.
   Who opposes Jeremiah in ch. 14 and why? What is wrong with their stance?

   How does Jeremiah respond to the opposition and what encouragement does God give him? Does that accord with your own experience?

Chs. 16–17: God spells out the challenge to Jeremiah.
   What does Jeremiah say is the sin of Judah that rouses God's anger?

   What does he say in ch. 17 is basically wrong with human nature?

Ch. 18: At the potter's house.
   What was Jeremiah's message that stirred opposition again?

   What is the gist of his prayer in vv. 19-23? Have you ever felt like praying something similar?

Chs. 19–20: In the stocks.
   What parallels do you find here between Jeremiah's and Jesus' experience?

   In what ways do their stories differ?

21.1 – 23.8: On the future of David's line.
Why was there no hope for Jerusalem through the Davidic kings of the day?

Jeremiah sees only judgment for the house of David, so what hope does he hold out for God's original promise to David?

23.9 – 25.38: On false prophetic views about the future.
From what Jeremiah says in 23.9-40, how would you hope to recognise a false prophet?

What hope does Jeremiah hold out for the exiles in chs. 24–25?

Chs. 26–27: Jeremiah's prophetic word on trial: how will the king respond to it?
How does Jehoiakim's attitude to Jeremiah differ from Hezekiah's to Micah and what does that matter anyhow?

How would you summarise Jeremiah's warning to king and priest in ch. 27?

Chs. 28–29: Prophet against prophet.
If you had been there listening to Jeremiah and Hananiah, how would you have judged which one spoke the word of the Lord?

What is the gist of Jeremiah's letter to the exiles?

....

REVIEW

This week's readings touch on two vast subjects:
• Firstly, the cost of standing for the word of God in persecution. What have you learned about God's encouragement to those called to speak his word in such times?

• Secondly, the problem of distinguishing the true word of God from the false. What have you learned about that?

What do you do when you feel like Jeremiah did in 20.9?

Week 11   *Heirs of the Prophets, Pages 113–20*

JEREMIAH'S PASSION AND NEAR-MARTYRDOM (Jeremiah 30–52)

In the story of Jeremiah's trials there are many reminders of Christ's sufferings. But there are also many points at which the story will touch your own life and experience: in the visions of hope for the future, in the challenge of preaching to unreceptive hearts, in personal rejection for the gospel, in seeing everything you hoped for destroyed. And still you know, as Jeremiah did, that you must continue to preach. At such times it is good to know you are not unique!

....

Chs. 30–31: Visions of restoration and the future beyond.
What hope does Jeremiah see for the future of the nation?

How is the prophecy in 31.31-4 fulfilled through Christ's ministry?

Chs. 32–33: Promises of restoration.
Why did Jeremiah buy his uncle's field? Have you ever known the challenge of putting your money where faith asks you to?

What future does Jeremiah see for the Davidic throne?

Chs. 34: Jerusalem's faithlessness even at the end.
Do you think it was an easy thing for Jeremiah to tell the king God's message in vv. 1-7? We pray for the gift of prophecy today, but will we have the courage to give his message?

What lesson for your own life do you take out of vv. 8-22?

Chs. 35–36: How will Zedekiah respond to the prophetic word?
How were the Rechabites faithful (ch. 35)? How does their story challenge you?

What are the signs of Jehoiakim's hardness against God's word in ch. 36?

Chs. 37–39: The prophetic word is rejected and Jerusalem falls.
What is Jeremiah's consistent advice to king and people in Jerusalem at this time?

What parallels with Jesus' story do you see in these chapters?

40.1 – 41.15: Gedeliah's community at Mizpah.
Why do you think the Babylonian commander set Jeremiah free?

Why was Gedeliah assassinated?

Chs. 41.16 – 44.30: Jeremiah in Egypt.
Why do you think the people rejected Jeremiah's word when they so strongly insisted he give it? Is it that we only hear what we want to hear?

Why did the people return to their superstitions? Why could they not see the hand of God in all that had happened?

....

REVIEW

Jeremiah's is in some ways a depressing story, a tale of constant rejection. Even those who recognised that he spoke from God, like Zedekiah and the leaders at Mizpah, would not act on his word. One man did serve him faithfully, but he also found it hard to do so:

Chs. 45: A disciple's lot!
How are we to receive such teaching as in v. 5 in our day when prosperity and victory teaching is so much in vogue?

When Jeremiah was first called to be a prophet, he probably saw what lay ahead, for he wanted to opt out (ch. 1). How are we to set his experience alongside Paul's injunction to 'eagerly desire spiritual gifts, especially the gift of prophecy' (1 Cor. 14.1)?

If God calls you to prophesy, what will you do?

Chs. 46–52 are omitted for lack of space. Their prophecies against foreign nations add little to the themes we have studied so far. You can read them without comments and questions.

Week 12   *Heirs of the Prophets, Pages 121–8*

GOD'S PLAN FOR ISRAEL AND THE NATIONS
(Zephaniah, Nahum, Obadiah, Habakkuk)

These four little books are very different from each other: Zephaniah speaks of judgment and beyond, like Amos or Isaiah; Nahum is a strong warning of the harsh judgment coming to Assyria; Obadiah is a short tirade against Edom's heartlessness; Habakkuk is a prophet's notebook telling of his search for the meaning of life in his times. All still have important things to say to us today.

....

Zeph. 1.1 – 2.3: The day of the Lord is near.
What is 'the day of the Lord' and what will happen on it?

What does Zephaniah say should be done to prepare for its coming?

Zeph. 2.4 – 3.20: Judgment and beyond.
What future awaits the nations? (Our present-day counterparts to the nations are unbelievers who oppose the work of God.)

What future awaits the faithful among God's people?

Nah. 1: His way is in the whirlwind and the storm.
Why do you think Nahum's vision of God is so violent?

Nahum's name means 'Comfort'. What comfort is there in ch. 1?

Nah. 2–3: The judgment on Nineveh.
What comfort is there for the Lord's people in these visions of harsh judgment on Assyria?

What does 3.1,19 suggest were the reasons for Assyria's judgment?

Obadiah: As you have done, it will be done to you.
   What was Edom's sin?

   What kind of sermon could you preach from this book?

Hab. 1–2: The righteous will live by his faith.
   What is Habakkuk's problem (ch. 1)?

   What has faith (2.4) to do with the questions he asks in ch. 1?

Hab. 3: Yet I will rejoice in the Lord.
   Why do you think God revealed himself to Habakkuk as a warrior?

   What enabled Habakkuk's questions of ch. 1 to be replaced by the faith and praise of 3.17-19?

....

REVIEW

   We all live today in an environment that is basically hostile to the preaching of the gospel of Jesus Christ, and so there is some similarity between our situation and that of Israel among the pagan nations. What encouragement for faith have you received out of this week's readings that might help you in a hostile setting?

   Write out some of the verses that have particularly spoken faith to you.

   How would you say Paul's teaching in Phil. 4.4-7 is similar to or different from the central message of these four prophets?

Week 13　　　　　　　　　　　　　　　　　　　　　　　*Heirs of the Prophets, Pages 129–35*

GOD'S GLORY AND JERUSALEM'S FAITHLESSNESS (Ezekiel 1–16)

Ezekiel's book is full of variety: stories, prophecies, allegories, visions, etc. Be ready for style changes from chapter to chapter, but remember the message is consistent: Jerusalem continues unfaithful. God therefore cannot stay in the city any longer. He must depart and hand her over to judgment (by invasion), not for destruction, but for radical discipline and purging. The message for us as individuals and for our society today remains the same and is clear.

....

Ch. 1: Ezekiel's vision of the Glory of God.
　Try drawing an outline sketch of what you imagine Ezekiel saw in his vision.

　What does such a vision tell you about God's nature.

Chs. 2–3: Ezekiel receives his call.
　How was Ezekiel to handle the stubbornness of his hearers?

　Why should a scroll with words of bitter judgment taste sweet to Ezekiel?

Chs. 4–7: Dramatic prophecies of Jerusalem's fate.
　What hope, if any, does Ezekiel hold out to the Israelites in his acted prophecies in chs. 4–5?

　How would you sum up his message in chs. 6–7?

Chs. 8–9: Idolatry in the temple.
　List the idolatries Ezekiel saw in the temple.

　What is God doing in ch. 9? Why does he have a mark put on the foreheads of some?

Chs. 10–11: God's Glory leaves Jerusalem.
What message is Ezekiel giving about Jerusalem through his vision of the departure of God's glory in ch. 10?

Outline the future hope expressed in ch. 11.

Ch. 12: Ezekiel dramatically prophesies the exile.
How would Ezekiel's dramatic actions have helped to open rebellious people's eyes that do not see?

What is your answer when people say to you things like the Israelites said to Ezekiel in vv. 22 and 27?

Chs. 13–14: He condemns false prophets and calls the elders to repent.
Are prophecies of 'Peace' always wrong? What is the danger in them?

In ch. 14 Ezekiel says Jerusalem is past redemption, though individuals can always be saved. How are we to recognise when a situation is beyond redemption? How did he recognise it?

Chs. 15–16: Jerusalem is a useless vine, an unfaithful bride.
How had God been good to Israel in the past and how had Israel responded (16.1-34)?

What was God going to do about that immediately (16.35-52) and in the more distant future (16.53-63)?

....

REVIEW

Ezekiel's preaching is very forthright. He does not mince his words about sin and judgment and is not afraid to back his prophecies in the most dramatic ways. What can we learn from him about confronting sin and proclaiming the gospel today, or do you think our world is so different that there is little we can learn from him?

What evidence is there that he was aware of God's love for Israel?

How are we to preach both judgment and love?

GOD'S JUDGMENT ON JERUSALEM AND THE NATIONS (Ezekiel 17–32)

The prophecies of judgment continue on from last week's and their message intensifies until the climax is reached in ch. 24, where Ezekiel is told he will prophesy no more until he hears the city has fallen. The prophecies against the nations in chs. 25–32 contain many interesting passages, but you can skip through them, for they do not add much to the aspects of the prophets' message we are studying here.

....

Chs. 17–18: The Lord's planting and individual responsibility.
How does Ezekiel show in ch. 17 that God's favour is more powerful than man's (Babylon's or Egypt's)?

The nation may be lost, but individuals need not be. What does God want for individuals and how are they to get it (ch. 18)?

Chs. 19–20: A lament and a historical survey.
In 20.1-29 what does Ezekiel say has been the essential nature of Israel's sin?

What does God propose to do about it in the short and the long term?

Ch. 21: Babylon the instrument of God's judgment.
How will the king of Babylon bring judgment on Jerusalem?

Can you think of any pagan power in this century that has been effectively used as God's sword of judgment on the church in this or any other country?

Chs. 22–3: The totality of Jerusalem's sin—Oholah and Oholibah.
The sins of the princes, priests, officials and prophets are still found among churchmen and statesmen, but who stands in the gap today (22.23-31)?

Oholibah should have learned the lesson from Oholah's judgment and repented. Is there anyone's suffering you need to learn from?

Ch. 24: The turning point.
  Explain the allegory of the cooking pot.

  Why was Ezekiel to react to his wife's death in such a strange way?

Chs. 25–28: Prophecies concerning foreign nations.
  What was the sin of the nations in chs. 25–26?

  What was the sin of Tyre and its king in chs. 27–28? (Note that 28.12-19 is often interpreted as reflecting the story of Satan's downfall in Eden.)

Chs. 29–32: More prophecies concerning foreign nations.
  What was Egypt's sin?

  What was to happen to her?

....

REVIEW

  You have been reading a lot about judgment over the past few weeks. How well have you understood the principles by which it operates? Try to answer the following questions in the light of what you have read, not just out of your own preconceptions.

  What is it that brings down the curse of God's anger?

  What is the Day of the Lord?

  Why does God act in judgment and what good does it do?

  Where do the prophets see God's mercy fitting in with his judgment?

  What is the point of a prophet forewarning about judgment?

  How does judgment fit in with God's promise to restore blessing to mankind through his chosen people?

Week 15   *Heirs of the Prophets, Pages 139–45*

THE RESTORED COMMUNITY AND THE NEW JERUSALEM (Ezekiel 33–48)

The judgment came, Jerusalem fell, and the prophet's role changed. He was still to be a watchman and still had to warn against sin and its dangers, but the future he saw was now of a totally different order. With the judgment past, it was time to look for restoration so that God's purposes for redemption could go on to fulfilment. His visions therefore probe beyond that immediate restoration down the centuries and even into ages in which we ourselves have not yet lived.

....

Ch. 33: Ezekiel's new appointment and the fall of Jerusalem.
Summarise Ezekiel's message in vv. 8-20.

What was wrong with the way the Israelites treated his words? How was he to view that?

Chs. 34–35: God's purpose to shepherd and protect his people.
What is wrong with the way shepherds and flock were behaving?

What is God's plan to shepherd and protect his people?

Chs. 36–37: The Lord's plans for Israel's future.
What did God say he would do for the Israelites when he brought them home (ch. 36)?

What does ch. 37 tell you about God's purposes in national revival?

Chs. 38–39: The Lord's plan for the future of the nations.
What elements in these chapters do you feel you have already lived through, or do you know other Christians have?

What elements do you feel relate entirely to the time of the end of history?

Chs. 40–42: The plan of the new temple.
Study the sketch of the temple in your Reading Guide and as you read these chapters draw your own sketch to help you get the feel of the temple better.

What is there in these chapters that tells you this is a vision from God you are dealing with, not just a human architect's plans?

Chs. 43–46: The temple springs to life.
Don't spend too much time trying to understand all the priestly laws, etc. Just try to get the feel of life in the temple. What was the difference between a Zadokite and a Levite?

What does the fact that God's glory came to reside in the sanctuary tell us about his relationship with his people? Today we have no stone temples, so where does God's glory reside now?

Chs. 47–48: The overflow from the temple into the land.
What is there about 47.1-12 that reminds you of the Garden of Eden?

What is there about the vision of the redistribution of the land that tells you Ezekiel's vision is idealistic and symbolic rather than practical?

....

REVIEW

Write a very brief, sketch outline (using only headings, if you wish) of the development of history after the exile as Ezekiel sees it in chs. 34–48.

What elements of that history do you believe have already come to pass?

What were the main aspects of his vision that thrilled you most?

Week 16 *Heirs of the Prophets, Pages 148–57*

PREPARING THE WAY FOR THE LORD (Isaiah 40–55)

This week there are no stories, only teaching that flows on smoothly from chapter to chapter: The exile is almost over. Get ready to move. God's judgment is past. He is coming to set you free, to restore you to your calling to be a light to the nations. Jerusalem will be rebuilt. God is doing a new thing. So wake up. Depart. Go serve the Lord. Zion has a glorious future. This prophet's message still has rich personal applications today.

....

Chs. 40–41: Comfort my people! Say, 'Here is your God!'
What are the 'good tidings' (v. 9) the prophet brings in ch. 40?

What encouragement is there in ch. 41?

Chs. 42–43: Israel is to be a light to the nations.
What is Israel's function to be (see esp. 42.6f)? What connection is there between that and our own Christian function today?

What, according to ch. 43, will God do to prepare Israel for that function?

Chs. 44–45: I am the Lord, and I say Jerusalem will be rebuilt.
What will God do that idols cannot (ch. 43)?

What do you learn from ch. 45 about God's power to do apparently impossible things in history?

Chs. 46–47: I am the Lord and there is no god besides me.
What is the essential message of ch. 46?

What do the Babylonians look to for their strength (ch. 47) and how far do people still look to the same things today?

Chs. 48–50: From now on I tell you new things.
Why, according to ch. 48, is it important to listen to the word of God through the prophets?

What reasons does 49.7 – 50.3 give for rejoicing?

Chs. 51–52: Awake! Depart! Proclaim, 'Your God reigns!'
What are the signs that deliverance is at hand?

What preparations do the people need to make for its coming?

52.13 – 53.12: The Lord's Servant.
Read 42.1-4; 49.1-6; 50.4-9 before 52.13 – 53.12, then explain how Christ's life fulfils these prophecies.

Chs. 54–55: Zion's Future Glory.
What kind of hope can God's people look forward to?

What kind of action does the teaching of these two chapters encourage you to take?

....

REVIEW

Have you ever had the sense that God is on the move, about to do something fairly dramatic, and that you need to get ready for it to happen? Perhaps you feel something of that sense now. What passages give you encouragement as you wait for God to act in your life?

What passages have especially spoken comfort and assurance to you?

What passages have challenged you to take action over some issue or some aspect of your life?

Week 17 — *Heirs of the Prophets, Pages 158–65*

RESTORING VISION AND PURPOSE (Haggai and Zechariah)

Haggai and Zechariah belong to the early years of the restored community after the exile. Much of their prophesying was intended to rouse faith, vision, morale and enthusiasm among the people who were struggling against difficult odds to rebuild their city and their lives. Much of their exhortation focuses on rebuilding the temple and maintaining the service of God, and so they have much to say to us today about our struggles to see our lives or ministries established.

....

Haggai: Work, for I am with you.
What does ch. 1 say to you about life's priorities?

What does ch. 2 say to you about God's provision when you get your priorities right?

Zech. 1–2: First to third visions of restoration.
What hope do these visions hold out for the people of Jerusalem?

These visions were addressed to a people who repented (1.2-6). What is the relationship between repentance and promises of blessing?

Zech. 3–4: Fourth and fifth visions
What personal encouragement do you take from the story of Joshua's encouragement in ch. 3?

What personal encouragement do you take from the story of Zerubbabel's encouragement in ch. 4?

Zech. 5–6: Sixth to ninth visions.
The visions of ch. 5 say God will purge the community of sin. If God does that, what is my responsibility in relation to sin?

What do the visions of ch. 6 tell you about God's purposes for the world?

Zech. 7–8: A call to live in repentance and the vision of blessing.

What does ch. 7 tell you about right attitudes in fasting?

'We have heard that God is with you' (8.23). What are the evidences of God's blessing outlined in ch. 8?

Zech. 9–11: The times of Messiah.

How many of the prophecies in these chapters find fulfilment in the life of Jesus?

What is there in these chapters that encourages you to rejoice today?

Zech. 12–14: The times of the end.

Chs. 12–13 contain things difficult to understand, but also matter echoed in the life of Christ. Where do you see such foreshadowings of Christ?

Ch. 14 also contains many strange things, but what in it particularly delights you?

....

REVIEW

Our fellowship was once involved in a building project without the resources to do it and so had to trust the Lord to provide at every stage. At that time we found Haggai and Zechariah invaluable, both as encouragement to the leaders to persevere in the work in faith, and to the rest of the fellowship to persevere in prayer and vision. It is not every day we erect buildings, but the principles are the same in handling any faith-objective in our Christian life and ministry. In what ways do Haggai and Zechariah encourage you?

How could you use their teaching to encourage your leaders?

How could you use their teaching to encourage your fellow Christians?

Week 18   *Heirs of the Prophets, Pages 165–77*

FINAL PREPARATION FOR THE LORD'S COMING
(Isaiah 56–66, Joel, Malachi)

We now come to some of the final aspects of the Old Testament prophetic vision. The teaching here about future glory, the age of the Spirit and the Lord's coming have richly inspired Christians down the ages and still today speak of the potential of our faith. Some of what they portray still lies in our future, but much of it is realisable through life in the Spirit as a Christian now.

....

Chs. 56–59: The prophet calls for repentance again.
   What do these chapters teach you about the continuing need for repentance?

   What do they point to as the central aspects of our faith?

Chs. 60–62: He reaffirms the vision of Zion's future glory.
   Many believe the portrait of life painted in chs. 60–61 should be reflected in today's churches. What aspects of it would you like to see reflected in your church?

   What does ch. 62 suggest we should do about seeing the vision fulfilled?

Chs. 63–64: He prays for God to come and fulfil the vision.
   What is the prophet praying for in ch. 63?

   Ch. 64 is often used as a prayer for revival. Why? Do you think it is suited for that purpose?

Chs. 65–66: God answers that the punishment will give way to glory.
   What do you think is the connection between the prophecies of judgment in 65.1-16 and the vision of future bliss in 65.17-25?

   Point out two or three things in ch. 66 that you find particularly faith-inspiring or encouraging?

Joel: I Will Pour out My Spirit.
What do chs. 1–2 suggest about the relationship between repentance and the gift of the Spirit?

What does ch. 3 say must happen in history after the Spirit is poured out?

Mal. 1.1 – 2.16: Why do you break faith?
What are the sins of the priests in 1.6 – 2.9? How far are they still a problem in our churches today?

How have the people broken faith in 2.10-16? How far do we still break faith in the same way today?

Mal. 2.17 – 4.6: Suddenly the Lord will come.
God's coming is in judgment, but there is a way to escape his wrath. What is that (2.17 – 3.18)?

Summarise the message of ch. 4.

....

REVIEW

There are plenty of prophecies in this week's readings that find some measure of fulfilment in the New Testament. List some of them and say how they were fulfilled.

Which prophecies from this week's readings have you seen fulfilled in your own life and experience?

Week 19 — *Heirs of the Prophets, Pages 180–94*

JESUS AND THE REBIRTH OF PROPHECY (Luke 1–12)

There are many different ways of reading the gospel story. For the purpose of this course look for signs of the work of the Holy Spirit and of prophetic and charismatic action in Jesus' ministry. Also bearing in mind that we are looking at Jesus as Prophet and that we as Christians are 'heirs of the prophets', keep asking how much of Jesus' prophetic ministry should be ours today.

....

Chs. 1–2: First stirrings of the prophetic Spirit.
Note all the times the Holy Spirit and prophecy are mentioned. What do you read that reminds you of the Old Testament prophets?

Samuel launched the old prophetic movement, Jesus the new. What links do you see between Mary and Jesus here and Hannah and Samuel in 1 Sam. 1–2?

Chs. 3–4: Jesus is attested as a prophet of the Lord.
Why do you think Jesus had to have the Holy Spirit descend on him before he started his ministry? Do we also?

What evidence is there in ch. 4 that the power behind Jesus' ministry was the Holy Spirit?

Chs. 5–6: Forming the team and first teaching.
What is there to suggest that it was charismatic activity among Jesus and his disciples that annoyed the religious of the day?

Is there anything in Jesus' sermon in 6.20-49 that reminds you of the teachings of the Old Testament prophets?

Ch. 7: Is he a prophet? 'Are you the one?'
The crowd recognise Jesus as 'a great prophet' (7.16). What in ch. 7 suggests he was?

Why do you think John the Baptist doubted? And the Pharisees?

Chs. 8–9: Ministry training and revelation.
What are the different effects Jesus' miracles have on people in ch. 8?

What did the disciples learn through their experiences in ch. 9?

Ch. 10: The ways of Kingdom mission.
What did the disciples learn through their mission?

What does v. 21 tell you about Jesus' relationship with the Spirit and the Father?

Ch. 11: The ways of the Spirit, of sin and of religion.
What do vv. 1-13 tell you about the connection between prayer and the Holy Spirit?

What are some of the attitudes in vv. 37-53 still found in the churches today?

Ch. 12: Right attitudes for the last days.
From this chapter list some of the attitudes we should be having today.

....

REVIEW

Briefly list the main prophetic traits you have discovered in Jesus' ministry.

Which of these traits should be found in Christian ministry today?

Which of them do you recognise from your own or your church's experience?

Week 20   *Heirs of the Prophets, Pages 194–200*

THE CHALLENGE AND CULMINATION OF THE PROPHET'S MINISTRY
(Luke 13–24)

As you read through Jesus' teaching and then the story of his last week, keep reminding yourself that in this course we are looking for the evidences of his prophetic/charismatic anointing. Other aspects of his ministry come to greater prominence as you read on, especially his kingship, but don't let that obscure the prophetic aspect, nor the fact that as heirs of the prophets he is our best prophetic example.

....

Ch. 13: Repent or perish.
   The Old Testament prophets laid challenges of obedience and faith before their hearers. What are the main challenges here?

   How would you describe from this chapter the prophetic heart of Jesus?

Chs. 14–15: Care for the poor, love the lost.
   What does Jesus ask us to do for the poor in ch. 14?

   What does Jesus ask us to do for the lost in ch. 15?

Chs. 16–17: The day has arrived, come now with repentance and faith.
   What does ch. 16 tell us about the challenge of entering the kingdom?

   What does ch. 17 tell us about the potential of faith?

Chs. 18–19: To Jericho and then to Jerusalem.
   In ch. 18, what kind of attitudes does Jesus commend?

   What are some of the signs in 18.31 – 19.48 that it was Jesus' charismatic power as much as his messiahship that excited people?

Chs. 20–21: Jesus' final challenge.
What and who does Jesus claim to be in the teaching in ch. 20?

Briefly outline the sequence of events foreseen in ch. 21.

Chs. 22–23: The Prophet's last hours.
List some of the prophetic/charismatic things Jesus did during his last hours.

Is persecution, even martyrdom, an inescapable part of a prophet's calling (cp. 13.33f)?

Ch. 24: Final preparation of the prophetic team.
Why do you think Jesus took his followers through the Bible again at this late stage (vv. 27,44f), as if in last minute preparation for something?

Is there anything in this chapter that suggests Jesus expected his disciples to become prophets too?

....

REVIEW

What aspects of Jesus' teaching did you perceive to be in the same vein as that of the Old Testament prophets?

What aspects of his ministry did you perceive to be prophetic/ charismatic?

What responses to his ministry did you perceive to be either positive or negative reactions to his charismatic anointing?

How far do you think reaction to his charismatic ministry was what led to his death?

How much of Jesus' ministry or suffering have you known in your own experience to result from the work of the Holy Spirit in your life?

What have you learned from this study that would encourage you to become more like Jesus the Prophet?

Week 21   Heirs of the Prophets, Pages 201–18

GROWTH OF THE CHRISTIAN PROPHETIC MOVEMENT
(Acts and Corinthians)

This week we arrive among Christians who, just like ourselves, are living in the New Covenant age and enjoying the fullness of the Spirit promised through the old covenants. Note, however, just how much their faith and experience are like those of Jesus and the ancient prophets. It is to such a life style we are still called, so see how much you can learn from them about how to live in the same Spirit today.

....

Acts 2 & 19.1-7: 'I will pour out my Spirit and they will prophesy.'
In what ways has the gift of the Holy Spirit made you a prophet or more like one?

Should we expect Christians today to answer the question in Acts 19.2 with a strong 'yes' and be able to show evidence to back up their answer?

Acts 3–4: Peter and John's miracle and their boldness.
Summarise Peter's sermon in ch. 3.

What do you learn from ch. 4 about the quality of life in the early church?

Acts 6–7: Stephen's dynamic witness and martyrdom.
Stephen was appointed to serve, not evangelise. So how was it that he made such an impact and stirred up such opposition?

What similarities do you see between Stephen's and Jesus' deaths?

Acts 8–9: Philip, Paul and Peter.
What does ch. 8 suggest about the connection between conversion and baptism in the Holy Spirit?

When was Paul baptised in the Spirit?

Acts 10–11: Peter with Cornelius and Barnabas at Antioch.
In what ways is Peter's anointing like that of the Old Testament prophets?

What was it that clinched the debate about Cornelius in Acts 11? What does that tell you about the significance of the Holy Spirit in Christian experience?

1 Cor. 2 and 2 Cor. 3: The general prophetic endowment.
Explain what the Holy Spirit reveals to us, according to 1 Cor. 2.

How is the veil lifted from our minds and what happens to us when it is (2 Cor. 3)?

1 Cor. 12–14: The gift of prophecy.
What is the relationship between the gifts of the Spirit, the body of Christ and love?

What, according to ch. 14, is the purpose of tongues and prophecy?

....

REVIEW

This week we have skipped hurriedly over many passages that are foundational to the understanding of Christians in the Charismatic and Pentecostal Movements of today. It is unfortunate that more time could not be spent on them, but our purpose has been mainly to see how New Testament Christianity is a continuity of the faith and experience of the Old Testament prophets, how we today are part of a continuous flow of God's purposes from earliest times, a work which has been headed up by prophetic men of the Spirit in every age. Such is the work we are still called to today.

How do the gifts of the Spirit help us to fulfil that calling?

How does the gift of prophecy in particular help us to fulfil that calling?

What particular aspects of the experience of these early prophetic/charismatic Christians do you think we still need to recover today?

Week 22 *Heirs of the Prophets, Pages 219–31*

THE FINAL PROPHETIC VISION OF HISTORY NOW AND TO COME
(Revelation 1–12)

With Jesus the history of God's redemptive purposes entered a new era. Through the gift of the Spirit, we already live with a foretaste of our eternal heavenly inheritance, equipped and empowered to do battle for God during this last phase of his war to win back the earth from sin and Satan. The battle is not yet over. Revelation gives us God's perspective on it and like all prophecy is written to encourage us in it. Read its vision to be encouraged. Don't let yourself get bogged down in its more puzzling elements.

....

Ch. 1: John tells of his vision of Jesus.
   What does John say is his purpose in writing?

   What does the vision of Jesus tell you about his relationship with the churches?

Chs. 2–3: The prophetic message to the Church.
   Note the emphasis on repentance. What kind of things are the churches asked to repent of?

   Note the emphasis on standing firm. What kind of things are the churches asked to hold on to?

Ch. 4: John enters God's throne-room in Heaven.
   What similarities do you see between John's vision in ch. 4 and Isaiah's in Isa. 6?

   Why do you think the door in heaven was standing open? And why do you think John speaks about 'seven spirits of God'?

Ch. 5: The Lamb receives a scroll from God's hand.
   What makes the Lamb worthy to take the scroll?

   What groups of people and creatures have you met in heaven in chs. 4–5 and what are they all doing?

Ch. 6: The Lamb begins to open the seals on the scroll.
What happens at the opening of the first four seals?

What happens at the opening of the fifth and sixth seals?

Ch. 7: John is granted refreshing views of heaven again.
What made 'these in white robes' different from everyone else John saw?

What personal encouragement do you take from this chapter?

Chs. 8–9: The seventh seal and the sounding of seven trumpets.
What parts of the world are affected by the sounding of the first four trumpets?

Why does God allow such monstrous things as described in ch. 9 to happen at all?

Chs. 10–11: Christian prophetic witness before the end.
The scroll of ch. 5 is the scroll of history. What is this 'little scroll' in ch. 10?

Amid all the strange symbolism of ch. 11, what happens to the prophetic Christian witnesses?

....

REVIEW

Most of what we have read this week relates to life as we now live it. The messages to the churches are still for us. Much of what happens when the seals are opened or the trumpets sounded is already happening in our world. The way the prophetic witnesses are treated is also frequently experienced.

What encouragement have you found in these chapters that would sustain you in faith in the midst of such times?

How do they challenge you about the state of your own faith?

Week 23   *Heirs of the Prophets, Pages 231–8*

THE LAST BATTLE AND THE END (Revelation 12–22)

We now leap forward to the end, to the last confrontation of God and evil, the re-establishment of God's kingdom on earth and the creation of a New Heaven and New Earth. The gist of this vision is in the Old Testament, but not with such detail. Remember as you work through some of the horrors of it, that its purpose is to encourage. That was also the purpose of the old prophecies against the nations. The battle with evil is a necessary prelude to the establishment of righteousness.

....

Chs. 12–13: Satan is thrown out of heaven and summons the beast.
Satan is unable to hurt the Church (the woman), Christ (the child) or Christians (the rest of the woman's offspring) in ch. 12. Why?

The two beasts in ch. 13 are imperial power and its political machinery. What causes men to reject God in favour of them?

Ch. 14: John is shown the forces of heaven ranged against the beast.
Why do the angels go out proclaiming the gospel at the last moment before the harvest?

What is the difference between the two harvests and what do they signify?

Chs. 15–16: The seven angels with the seven bowls of God's wrath.
How do the first six plagues differ from what you read about in chs. 6 and 8–9?

What happened at the pouring out of the seventh bowl?

Ch. 17: The beast's identity is revealed.
Why do you think John was 'astonished' in v. 6?

Do you see the power of the woman and the beast at work anywhere in our world today?

Chs. 18–19: Babylon's fall and the victory procession of heaven.
How do the kings and merchants react to Babylon's fall? Would you react in anything like the same way?

Heaven reacts with loud Hallelujahs. Why?

Ch. 20: The Millennium and the Last Judgment.
Who precisely is to rule on earth during the Millennium?

What is the difference between 'the books' and 'the book of life'?

Chs. 21–22: The new heaven and new earth, and the new Jerusalem.
What particularly do you find attractive about John's vision of the New Jerusalem?

What aspects of it remind you of the garden of Eden?

....

REVIEW

During this course you have read about prophets fighting to restore God's kingdom work through revival preaching, sometimes with amazing success, sometimes having to accept God's judgment. But through it all they saw that God would establish a new phase of kingdom work through Christ and the outpouring of his Spirit and that that would initiate the final thrust towards the ultimate redemption of earth. As we live in this last phase now, the vision of Revelation encourages us to stand firm in our faith and look forward with hope.

How has its vision encouraged you?

What is the point of being a prophet yourself?